"This book provides unique information that empowers the individual to make important personal decisions regarding his or her future."

—American Cancer Society

"In his death, Mr. Manuel has made an enormous contribution to others' lives. This book offers compassionate, but practical suggestions. Using journaling as a tool, the book offers invaluable advice and support to those facing death, noting that preparation is an ultimate act of love toward the survivors."

—Teresa Vaughn
Attorney at law, Hospice Volunteer
Denver, CO

"Izzy Justice has captured Randy Manuel's style, message and spirit. He has created a sensitive work of guidance and hope for people who find themselves in this stage of life."

—Irene Manuel
Wife of Randy Manuel
Charlotte, NC

Is Today The Day?

Is Today The Day?

Izzy S. Justice

iUniverse, Inc.

New York Lincoln Shanghai

Is Today The Day?

iUniverse, Inc.

For information address:
iUniverse, Inc.
2021 Pine Lake Road, Suite 100
Lincoln, NE 68512
www.iuniverse.com

ISBN: 0-595-27732-2

Printed in the United States of America

To my wife, Stephanie, who continues to teach me the joys of living. And to Randy Manuel—I pray I have captured his singular message for the use of many.

Contents

Acknowledgement

Irene Manuel was instrumental in helping me keep true to Randy Manuel's life and story. There were several interviewees, cancer survivors, care volunteers, editors and researchers who lent their time and creativity to this project. I extend a special note of gratitude to the editing of Andrew Arnone.

Foreword

Gary Frenette M.D. Ph.D.

I had the distinct honor of being Randy's medical oncologist throughout his illness. Anyone who thinks that being a cancer doctor is a depressing job never knew Randy Manuel. Randy had a zest for life that was infectious and wisdom about death that cannot be acquired but must be earned. Randy was courageous, humorous, sometimes challenging, and always inspirational.

The advances in cancer are not only measured by new medicines, scans or screening tests. Randy understood that the end of our life's journey is one we will ultimately all share. We need to constantly refine our care for people in this phase of life. Randy's contribution ehelps to shepherd us through his intimate and personal journey so that we can benefit from his experience.

This book is unique, ground-breaking, and inspirational. In giving us information about dying, it teaches us important lessons about life. When a cancer diagnosis strips away the veneer of everyday life, we rely on faith, family and friends for strength and support. With this book and in so many other ways, Randy left this world a better place for having been here. The book along with its companion video is a wonderful tribute to a man who dedicated his final years to making the journey easier for all of us to follow. We thank you and miss you.

From the Author

It is not too often that one is presented with an opportunity to use one's craft for the greater good. Mankind in general, and artists in particular, often pray for both the inspiration to augment their trade and to have that enhanced manifestation of skill be put to use for the general well-being of our race and evolution.

It is with this honor that I accepted the challenge of writing about a man I concede I never met, and about a subject that is as ancient as man himself—our mortality and the preparation for it.

How can I do Randy Manuel's life story any justice? I asked myself. How can I describe his last months not having witnessed them? How can I take his story and allow not just Stage IV cancer patients—but all terminally ill—to benefit from his passion to leave something behind for others that befall such a terrible realization in a suddenly constricted timeframe? What creative lens should I wear—if any—as author? How much creativity can I use without compromising a powerful message? I wrestled with these questions for many months and resigned with this intriguing proposition: In Randy's last rite of passage, a unique gift was presented to us—simply unwrap it for others to learn from and enjoy.

So, in the humble spirit of humanity, I embark with you on a journey to explore an unsettling and nebulous experience—preparing for death. Much has already been written about this subject. It could even be argued that this anxiety is at the very core of philosophy, religion, and other schools of thought. So what is in this book that is different? What can I, a 21st century author, tell you that you don't already

know, or cannot find in another book or video or Internet website? If
you or someone you love is dying, why should you bother to read this?

I offer the following responses to these good questions:

- Randy Manuel was a special and unique man. When he was
  diagnosed with Stage IV cancer, he found very little information
  on this final stage, and that which did exist was very difficult to
  access. It was as though everyone gave up in the final days of
  their illness and just waited for death. Randy dedicated his last
  few months to work on this project in order that others similarly
  diagnosed would have something he did not.

- This is not just a book you read—you are asked to participate,
  too. The questions asked throughout the book will help you, the
  patient or the loved one, to cope with an extremely difficult and
  sensitive vortex of complex emotions. Distracting yet important
  decisions must be made, and any way to insert clarity into this
  process should be considered. The experience of the "doing" is
  unique and, hopefully, worthy of your time.

- The information you capture and discover as a result of
  responding to the questions will become invaluable during the
  shortened timeframe you suddenly have before you. You will
  need to share your responses with many people many times
  over; however, your schedule and commitments will not extend
  you the luxury of having quality time with all these people. By
  allowing people to read your written responses, you allow yourself an alternate "forum" to say things that you do not feel comfortable verbalizing.

- This book, unlike other sources of information on death and
  dying (which I encourage you to read and explore), is not
  intended to be a dry statistical "one-stop-shop" approach to this
  matter. Rather its intention is to complement your knowledge
  base and to help you better manage your emotions. And perhaps
  more importantly, this book will help you to better manage
  your last precious weeks and months with those you love.

I urge you to take advantage of this book—complete it so that it becomes *your* book—something that you can leave behind or use to reflect and learn once your loved one has journeyed on. You may even want several copies for family members to fill out to compare responses and process collectively—for these are the conversations you will cherish the most.

Because of the sensitive nature of this book, the complexity of the subject, and questions being asked, this book is intentionally short. But do not be fooled, this book may take you significantly longer to complete than you think.

As part of the research for this book, I attended several support group sessions and found a tremendous thirst amongst participants to have quality conversations. Although I did not actively participate in these sessions, I inferred that the participants had had enough of the casual talk that they spent their lives mastering. This book might help you identify what some quality topics for conversations could be.

Finally, I wish to acknowledge that the experience of mortality is difficult and profound. I salute you and admire the strength and courage it will take to go through this journey. You have been given a reason to explore perhaps the greatest mystery of all—the hearts and souls of each other. I urge you not to waste this special time of your existence.

Introduction

Stage IV cancer is the final stage of cancer as currently defined by contemporary western physicians. Below is a description of each of the four stages:

- Stage I or "local" cancers have been diagnosed early and have not spread

- Stage II cancer has spread into surrounding tissues but not beyond the location of origin

- Stage III or "regional" cancer has spread to nearby lymph nodes

- Stage IV or "distant" cancers have metastasized—or spread to other parts of the body and are the most difficult to treat

At Stage IV, many patients have only weeks or months left to live. The focus shifts from treatment for recovery to treatment for pain reduction in anticipation of death.

Randall Charles Manuel was diagnosed with Stage IV cancer in Charlotte, North Carolina, on January 28, 1999. Randy suffered from breast cancer—a form of cancer traditionally associated with women and somewhat uncommon in men. He chose not to be told the amount of time he had left, although his family was made aware of an approximate six-month timeframe. He died on July 22, 2001. A brief chronology of his life and important events are included at the end of this section.

Slade Goldstein, a television producer and friend of Randy, was hired to produce a video documentary on Stage IV cancer with Randy as the star. To this end, the two developed a warm relationship and began to collaborate on how to capture the necessary information that others in Stage IV might find helpful.

Slade Goldstein captured many hours of video with Randy, the American Cancer Society, Hospice, his family, his physician, and other important people in his life. On one occasion, Randy invited several of his closest friends to participate for several hours as Slade videotaped their discussion. Randy answered any and all questions his friends asked him and insisted there be no constraints on the questions. The experience was unforgettable for Randy, Slade, and the friends. After all of these exchanges were captured on video, it was then suggested that a book be written to complement the documentary. This is that book.

The format is unique. There are no chapters in this book—just topics for thought, discussion, and writing. Each topic begins with several paragraphs of direct and minimally-edited transcription of Randy's comments and responses during the session with his friends.

This is followed by paragraphs of interpretation and key learning statements. At the end of each topic, you, the reader, will be asked several questions and provided space to write your response. Some of the questions may appear repetitive—this is by design. True progress is always an iterative process. Upon completion, you will have two stories—Randy's and yours.

Writing is perhaps the best way to process and sort out competing and complex thoughts in your mind. It is also the best way to stay focused as you involve many kinesthetic parts—your brain to think, your eyes to read, your hands to write. The act of writing makes you a captive audience and significantly reduces intruding thoughts. Writing is also a confidential. You can sort out your thoughts before speaking about them. If you still feel uncomfortable writing or are unable to, then pause during the questions, close your eyes, and think through your answers or ask someone to help you write them. It is imperative that you make an effort to write your responses. The questions have been carefully prepared and sequenced so that there is a logical order and progression. Make every effort to complete each question before proceeding to the next.

If you only read, you will learn. If you read and write, you will learn and benefit. If you read, write, and share, many important people in your life will benefit. If you read, write, share and act upon your own resulting conclusions, you will make invaluable use of your limited time with your loved ones.

Randall Charles Manuel

October 5, 1943	Born in Flint, Michigan. First child of Wilbur and Helen Manuel
1952–1959	Davidson, Michigan. Lived on 80-acre farm with parents, brother, two sisters, grandmother and grandfather
1962–1966	Flint Junior College, United States Air Force
April 16, 1966	Married Irene Lordan in St James, NY.
	Had three daughters: Kristine (1967), Kelly (1968) and Laura (1969). At death had seven grandchildren
1973–1999	Founder and President of Telecommunications Software Inc., a private company specializing in telephone network software
1999–2001	Volunteer for American Cancer Society (ACS), Buddy Kemp Caring House, and Carolinas Medical Center
Hobbies	Golf, photography, music and model boats
Service	Established two Stage IV support groups in Charlotte, NC, and had a starring role in the documentary *Is Today The Day?*

Topic 1
The Discovery

I had taken my daily shower and was toweling off when I noticed an indentation on my chest. I thought to myself, I must be getting older. I showed it to Irene, my wife, and she suggested I get it checked. I made an appointment with my primary care physician for the next day—Thursday I think it was.

So I went to the doctor, and he felt around the area, and he could immediately feel a tumor that was there. He said he was going to send me to two places—a surgeon for a biopsy and to get a mammogram. This was all strange for a man to hear, and the spot never really hurt or anything.

The biopsy is key. They use a thin needle, and they find a spot where the tumor is and extract a piece and put it under a microscope. No matter what type of cancer you think you may have, you must have a biopsy. I was fortunate to have the test done immediately and subsequently meet with my doctor that afternoon. He gave me the news that I had male breast cancer.

My stomach kinda went upside down. I tried to gather myself, and being the optimist that I am, I asked the doctor, "Ok—let's do something about it; let's fight it." I like the term "cancer fighter" as opposed to "cancer survivor."

Irene was there with me and all of a sudden I began to think about mortality. I mean I was 54 and I thought, "I'm gonna have the 50s, right? I expect to be in the 60s and 70s, right?" I mean I was looking at a different timeframe now—a shorter increment of life. I started to worry about how to conserve time.

I had surgery two weeks later. I just wanted it out of me. In terms of worrying about whether it was going to come back—yeah, that was my first worry. Then I worried about going back to work, but I really wasn't worried about dying of cancer at that point.

Then last year I was diagnosed with Stage IV. So I said to the doctor, "OK, now what? What do we do now? What treatment now?" And he looked at me and said, "Randy, this is it. There is no treatment for this stage."

When I went to Stage IV, two things happened right way. First, I went into clinical depression. It feels like a whirlpool just sucking you in, and you have no choice because you see death right ahead and you know it's going to happen. Second, I went to a psychologist and started taking medication for it.

◆   ◆   ◆

The time of discovery can be one of the more frightening experiences you may ever encounter—both as a patient and as a loved one. A flock of emotions inexplicably converge in your mind without pretense. The shock factor alone can often lead to significant disassociation from friends and family, preventing you from getting out of the immediate abyss. Be prepared for this time of confusion. And know that despite its chaotic feel, it is normal.

After some time has elapsed, the experience of the "discovery" of the terminal illness can become a wonderful icebreaker for communication purposes. When you tell another about this unfortunate experience and the emotions associated with it, it often gives the audience (a person or persons) license to go through those same emotions, which they may well do. Allowing them access to your initial reaction is a comfortable way of helping them figure out how they can help you.

◆   ◆   ◆

Describe your discovery:

_____

_____

_____

_____

Was anyone else present? What was his or her reaction?

_____

_____

_____

_____

What was the doctor's recommendation?

_____

_____

_____

_____

Where did you go after the news? What did you do? Who else did you inform?

_____

_____

_____

_____

What would you have wanted that you did not receive or have during the discovery?

_____

_____

_____

_____

What about your reaction would you change if you could?

_____

_____

_____

_____

Make a list of people with whom you need to communicate. (You will use this information in the latter part of the book to develop a communication plan.)

_____

_____

_____

_____

As other people react to your news, what specifically would you want them to know?

_____

_____

_____

_____

Family and friends are going to ask, "What can I do?" What will your response be?

_____

_____

_____

_____

List demographic information you want to keep for yourself or your loved ones:
Date of Discovery: _____
Primary Physician: _____
   contact number: _____
Primary Hospital: _____
   contact number: _____

Location of Medical Records: _____
Names and Numbers of Immediate Family:

_____

_____

_____

_____

_____

_____

Topic 2
Mortality

I was afraid of it most because it was just scary. It's like, Oh golly, I guess I am a lot closer than I thought now…passing away. I wondered what I would go through before I died—I mean what would happen to my body physically and what will pain be like?

I think many times the anticipation of death is much worse than the actual fact that it is going to happen. You go from thinking about it often during the day to some days not thinking about it much at all.

Those who fight it will last longer than those who don't. Those who roll over and say, "Well—it is what it is." Well, I think that shortens the amount of time they might have.

I am not worried about my daughters as much. I mean they have their husbands and kids—I worry about Irene. I am leaving her alone. We spent over 30 years together. What will she do when she sees or hears something that reminds her of me? That makes me very sad.

But this documentary project is a gift—this time has made me closer to the people I love than I ever imagined. I have seen the best in people and friends.

◆　　　◆　　　◆

Death is the ultimate mystery and has been since the advent of time and man. And in no way can this book attempt to make any sense of it.

However, Randy's brief but powerful comments regarding mortality only underscore the need for you to come to your own sense of peace *with* it—which is different from making sense *of* it.

Making peace with death simply implies that you have spent time thinking about it, have talked about it with those who matter to you, and have come to accept it so that your remaining time with your loved ones can be as wonderful as possible. The sign that you have made peace with it is in your ability to transfer your energy from anger and despondency to a conscious effort to optimize the remaining time with meaningful dialogue and experiences with the people close to you. If you begin to see the remaining time as a gift or an opportunity to demonstrate ultimate compassion and altruism, then you have made peace with it. You may want to ask family or friends to be honest with you and reflect if you appear to be at this stage, for you can often mislead yourself to easier but false conclusions.

Reading the insights of others can also help alleviate anger and despondency. Most libraries carry an extensive amount of information on this subject, covering a gamut of perspectives. You'll know which one might resonate with you. You are also encouraged to explore your faith as this can be a wonderful home for your new, albeit rudely-awakened and uninvited thoughts.

Making peace with death is an important first step in maximizing both the amount and quality of your remaining time. Randy captured this message in a powerful statement: "Life is not fair, but you can be."

◆   ◆   ◆

What scares you about mortality?

_____

_____

_____

_____

What are the names of people who might help you approach mortality?

_____

_____

_____

_____

What are the major questions you have regarding death?

_____

_____

_____

_____

How much time do you have left? Make a list of things that you want to see, people you want to meet, and things you want to do:

_____

_____

_____

_____

_____

_____

_____

_____

What could be some positive impacts of this experience? Can you help someone else because of your experience?

_____

_____

_____

_____

Write a brief paragraph describing your understanding of mortality, so that others may read it and understand how you have made peace with it.

_____

_____

_____

_____

_____

Is there a sign you want to establish with your loved ones to indicate that you want to discuss death? _____

_____

_____

What are some other ways you can make peace with death? _____

_____

_____

_____

Topic 3
Support System

I really don't like the phrase, "Well, if you have a good attitude, you know everything is going to be fine." Well, I'm sorry, but too many people died from this disease with the best attitudes in the world—that good attitude is not the difference.

Hospice is the most powerful thing that you can have. I mean they can do hundreds of little things for you. And they are volunteers—about 150-170 of them in Charlotte. They know this stuff.

I was in a wheelchair and it was getting difficult for me to get in and out of my house. Building a ramp is an expensive proposition during this time. Apparently, there are volunteers that contract with Hospice that build ramps all the time at cost. And so they helped build me one over a weekend.

When I first thought of Hospice, I did it for my wife, Irene. Because there's a lot of strain (as you can imagine) on the caregiver—a tremendous amount—it cannot be underestimated whatsoever. I didn't think Irene was having that much trouble, but she was. This definitely took some strain off her. There are just no minuses to Hospice—it's all plusses.

In fact the whole idea of this video session came from a hospice volunteer. He thought I could make a videotape for an attorney. I didn't like that. Then he said we could do a videotape for my family and I didn't like that either. But then I thought we could do one on Stage IV cancer since there is so little information at this stage.

Write this toll-free number down—(800) ACS-2345—it's the number of the American Cancer Society. There is someone on the other line there 24-7 who can offer a great deal of information and support to you. I got a lot of good literature from them.

Another thing is support groups. I get strength from the people who are there. When I got to Stage IV, I looked for a support group and there was none. Well, every person who dies of cancer goes through Stage IV—so how come there's no support group?

I had an intuition that some of these support group people would turn out to be genuine friends because we were in the same boat. It is so true.

There was one guy—Kevin (I'm sorry I can't remember his last name.) He passed away in October. I would see him at the support group and I would say, "Hey, Kevin, how ya doing?" He'd say, "Hey Rand—how's it going?" We would kid that whoever died first, the other would go to their funeral. When he died, it was my honor and pleasure to go to his funeral.

Another rewarding experience with Kevin was that he liked planes, and I liked to build model boats. He told me about a particular plane that he liked and I went to a hobby shop and sure enough it was there. I bought it and took it to Kevin's apartment one day, and we took out the box of tools I brought and starting building this thing. Before he died, we finished it. I mean how good does it make me feel that I could do a little thing like that and it meant the whole world to him? It wasn't easy but I was better for having known that man.

The bond in support groups is very powerful, especially in Stage IV. You can imagine that at other stages, people go for a short time because many beat it. But here, that's it—we're not going anywhere. At the Stage IV group, you're looking at the end. You look around the room, see who is there, how they are doing, and you want them to do well and be there the next session. Believe me, and don't take this the wrong way, but it definitely helps in your mind when you look across the room and see someone who is in twice as much pain as you. It surprised me to see the physical deterioration of the body as you got closer to dying.

Another good thing about support groups is that it gave Irene some free time, and funny thing is, she developed a support group with one of the other wives of one guy in my support group. After dropping us off, they would go get coffee together and talk about us! You know I read somewhere that those in a support group live twice as long as those not in one.

◆   ◆   ◆

There is a reason this topic is entitled "Support System" and not "Support Group." A support system is a much broader term encompassing the many dimensions about Stage IV as opposed to a support group that serves a single, albeit good, purpose. Other dimensions of the support system will be discussed in proceeding topics. Family and friends are clearly critical. In addition, the lawyers, accountants, financial planners, funeral home experts, ACS, websites, and other literature all also comprise the support system.

It is imperative that you think of your support as a system—each part fulfilling a specific need during this process. It will be tremendously rewarding for you and your loved ones to spend the necessary time upfront figuring out what you need from whom and then allowing that part of the system to meet its obligation with compassion. It indeed is a win-win proposition—you need help and they want to help.

There are several books written by organizations such as Hospice Net (www.hospicenet.org) and Hospice volunteers. At the end of this section, there is a list of recommended books on this subject, including websites for more information on support systems.

You are encouraged to read these and also explore the concept of hospice assistance. Their motto is: "Hospice adds life to years not years to life." Remember, you should not tackle this journey on your own. This is not the time to be a hero. Asking for help is not a sign of weakness or your inability to love your loved one. It is perhaps the best thing you can do to free up some time to manifest your love. As a caregiver, be prepared for exhaustion—emotionally, intellectually, spiritually, and physically. You will be drained at the end of each day.

The following is a sequence of Irene Manuel's account of a typical day taking care of Randy:

- Wake up early and get dressed
- Bathe, dress, and feed Randy
- Hospice visit
- Transfer from bed to wheelchair to car
- Go for drives to look at furniture, to drop off at hospital or support group meetings, or eat out. (Randy and Irene always enjoyed eating out and wanted to maintain that tradition.)
- Visit daughters' homes and grandchildren (It would be difficult for Randy to visit their homes because of his wheelchair. Not all the homes had ramps.)
- Rest in the afternoon
- Undress and prepare for bed and TV
- Sleep—if possible (Sleep was a luxury as sometimes Randy would sleep and other times he would not. Irene used to say she slept with one eye open.)

Somewhere in this schedule, a living had to be earned, bills had to be paid, people had to be updated and normal house chores had to be done. You can see what a daunting challenge this was.

Support groups are indeed an invaluable mechanism both during and after a shortened life experience. Irene still keeps in touch with one of the spouses of the deceased from the support group. This contact provides incomparable support to complement her other relationships with family and friends who perhaps have not lost a significant other.

For Randy, creating Stage IV support groups is his legacy. He found a way to keep living through the many institutions he established, which support people even after his death. This book is yet another testament to his legacy.

You have no idea what you will hear in these support groups, who you will meet or what you will feel like saying. But chances are very high that either you will benefit from it or someone else will benefit from your story. You are encouraged, as a fighter or as a significant other, to seek out a group and make it a part of your support system.

◆   ◆   ◆

In the space below, put your name in the middle circle of the support clock. In each of the small circles, write down all the names of people or groups of people or institutions that either comprise your support system or should comprise your support system. Please take your time creating this system.

My Support System

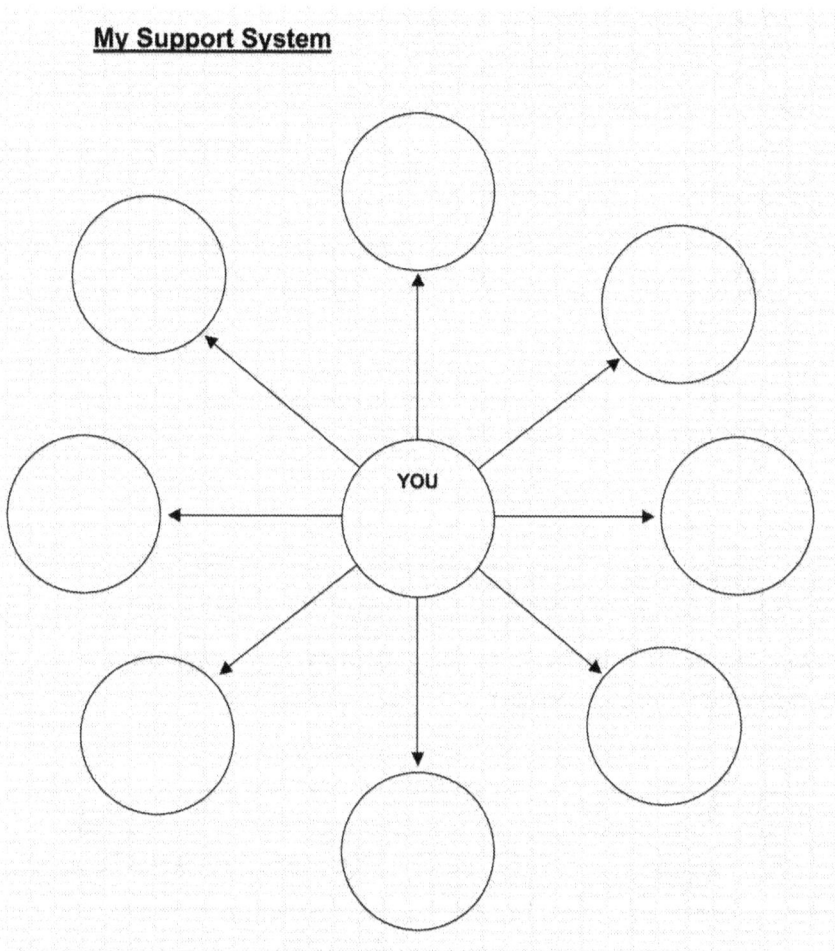

Describe in detail a typical day for you.

_____

_____

_____

_____

Based on your response above, go back to your support system clock and add additional areas where you might need assistance.

Make a list of possible contributions you can make to enhance the lives of others in your support system.

_____

_____

_____

_____

What legacy do you want to leave behind regarding both your illness and your final months?

_____

_____

_____

_____

_____

_____

_____

Recommended Reading List:

Choosing How To End, by Lynn Woodland

Cries of the Dying Awaken Doctors to a New Approach, by Sheryl Gay Stolberg

Death: The Final Stage of Growth, by Dr. Kubler-Ross
The world-renowned psychiatrist, whose pioneering work identified the five stages of terminal illness, shows how we come to terms with the idea of death.

What Does Someone Dying Need?, by Rex Winsbury

A Dying Person's Guide To Dying, by Roger C. Bone, M.D.

Final Gifts: Understanding the Special Awareness, Needs, and Communications of the Dying, by Maggie Callanan and Patricia Kelley

The Hospice Choice: In Pursuit of a Peaceful Death, by Marcia Lattanzi-Licht, Galen W. Miller, and John J. Maloney

Hospice Concepts: A Guide to Palliative Care in Terminal Illnesses, by Shirley Ann Smith
A U.S. consultant overviews hospice care philosophy, history, goals, interdisciplinary team approach, grief and bereavement concepts, spiritual care, pain management, legal and ethical issues, and the Medicare hospice benefit. Includes chapter tests with answers.

Recommended Websites on Support Groups:

- www.vitaloptions.org
- www.cancerhopenetwork.org

Topic 4
Taking Care of the Mundane

There's a lot I don't know about insurance; what's important at this time is to go to the person who represents you and say, "What are we going to do here?" They're certainly not going to be able to get you more insurance because you have cancer but you want to take an assessment of where you stand financially with insurance. Find someone in the insurance industry—a friend of a friend—anyone who understands this stuff because I certainly did not.

I was very pleased with one of the things that had happened through the accountant that I had a long time ago. I had been paying my premiums for disability insurance. What happens is that if you ever get disabled and can't work, then long-term disability is tax free, which means you can almost double the coverage. So if you were supposed to get $1,000 a month, you would not be taxed on it and in effect get twice what you expected.

Please get disability insurance—if not for yourself then for your loved one. I always thought that you would only use it when you got into an accident; I never thought about it in relationship to cancer. You have to find a way to make it one of the top things that you spend your money on and not buy a new car as often or whatever it is.

I had my own small business, and you know how small businesses are risky. I was just lucky that I had taken the insurance options that I did, which has made my life so much easier now. I tell you I would be in a world of hurt if I had to depend on social security. What happens with social security is that it is deducted from your insurance policies if you have more than one *long-term disability policy. But what you can do to avoid this is take an option where that won't happen, and most people don't realize that—I certainly did not until it actually happened. Whatever social security gives you—$800-$1,200 a month—won't take you far, so don't plan to rely on this.*

There's no doubt that cancer can be financially devastating. No one talks about this, but it's sad when entire families get financially ruined in addition to losing a loved one. I have heard of some senior citizens taking their lives to avoid the financial burden on their children or loved ones.

I strongly recommend that you get a lawyer, accountant, or a financial planner who can help you take inventory of everything you own. Get them to help you evaluate your entire situation and then you can plan accordingly. Don't try and do this yourself because you can't possibly remember all the policies or contracts or investments you made and their viability to your current situation.

Also make a will. It is not expensiveonly a couple hundred dollars. Please have one because if you don't, you're going to have some unfortunate and unexpected things happen to you, such as not being able to pass all the money to your heirs like you thought. I'm not an expert at this, but there are several wills—power of attorney and living wills and things like that.

◆   ◆   ◆

All of what Randy talked about is very important. And clearly, by the time a person is diagnosed with cancer, it is virtually impossible to get any type of insurance. So the message is two-fold.

First, for the general public, the disability policies Randy describes, and many others, are all made available by most employers and nearly all insurance companies. They are relatively inexpensive and you can only hope that you never have to use them. Serendipity has all the cards here, and you can be prepared for whatever she holds by preparing financially before such traumatic experiences occur. Most financial planners offer a free consultation regarding your finances; it would be advantageous to take advantage of this service. You are also encouraged to use "Scenario-Based Planning." Think about worse case scenarios and ask your planner if, based on your current financial portfolio, you would be able to survive the scenario. Change your scenarios to your significant other or children and ask the same questions: "What would happen if…?"

In most cases, you will find that you can make significant improvements to your coverage without incurring significant costs, certainly nothing that will compromise your current lifestyle. This is a classic no-brainer—you have almost nothing to lose and everything to gain.

Second, for those already diagnosed and currently living through this experience, taking inventory with the help of the experts is a "must do." Check your support system for people who could help or offer recommendations of other people who could help. The fine print in all the contracts and policies you have signed is a foreign language to most of us, but not to the experts. They can, at best, save you from spending on items you thought you needed, and, at worst, give you a clear picture of your financial landscape so you can journey your last few months with the most accurate information.

Randy's comments regarding a will are also worth serious consideration. Wills are very simple to draft and do not have to be redone on a regular basis unless you have significant changes in your decision regarding your family, heirs, and value of life. Again, look at your support clock and find someone who can refer you to someone who can legally draft such a document. Please note that simply taking a piece of paper and jotting down your last wishes does not constitute a legally binding will and could easily be contested.

At the end of this section are a list of websites that offer free access to documents, templates and reference material to help you navigate through your requirements.

Randy was lucky. He had his own small business, and because of the inherent risk with small businesses, he chose to hedge against his potential risks. We don't know if he would have made the same decisions if he worked for Corporate America where the only time most people think of benefits is the day they're hired. Randy chose wisely but wanted to make sure others do not have to rely on luck to have financial viability and security during what is already a trying time.

◆   ◆   ◆

Make a list of all your current insurance policies and write the name and number of someone who can review these for you.

_____

_____

_____

_____

Make a list of additional policies you think you may need.

_____

_____

_____

_____

Make a list of all your financial assets and next to each one, write the name of someone who can review it for you. Is there a lawyer, accountant, or financial planner you know who can provide you with a template (or questionnaire) to fill out to better capture your assets?

_____

_____

_____
_____
_____
_____
_____
_____

If you have any wills, how many do you have and where are they?

_____
_____
_____
_____

What additional wills do you think you may need? Who can you contact to make sure you have all the necessary wills?

_____
_____
_____
_____

If you do not have a will, who can you get to help you with one?

_____
_____
_____
_____

Return to your support system clock and add names from the above exercises to it.

Recommended websites for counsel on wills:

American Medical Association
http://www.ama-assn.org/public/booklets/livgwill.htm

The Memorial Hospital
www.thememorialhospital.com/tmhc.nsf/View/Advanced
Directives
www.thememorialhospital.com/tmhc.nsf/View/LivingWill
www.thememorialhospital.com/tmhc.nsf/View/LivingWill
#POA

Florida Department of Health and Human Services
www.fdhc.state.fl.us/MCHQ/Health_Facility_Regulation/
HC_Advance_Directives/adv_dir.pdf

www.wmhinc.org/patient%20info/livingwill.htm

www.wmhinc.org/patient%20info/durablepoa.htm

Topic 5
The Last Rites

This is one of those topics that you can choose to face or not. One of the things I cannot face is going out and buying my own plot, you know what I mean? The place I will be buried. I just can't do it, but Irene can. All I told her was that I wanted to be near her dad whom I was very close to. I also have not made a decision on a casket because it's another thing I can't do.

But there are a lot of other things I can decide on like the memorial service—the music, the pallbearers, you know. I do believe that you will be doing your family a large favor by documenting these last wishes, especially with little things that are important to you that you want others to have.

You'd be surprised how little you have that's really worth much. It's true. You may have the money in the bank and this and that and you may have a car, but what else after that? So I sat down with Irene one day and we talked about the watch going here and the ring going there, and I think it was very, very healthy and very key because we all know that there are lots of people trying to grab things once someone dies. If you document this stuff and sign it, then you can avoid these problems.

◆　　　◆　　　◆

Indeed, these last rites are perhaps the most emotional decisions you will have to make during this time. Planning your funeral can be one of the most powerful and rewarding experiences of your entire life. It should be noted that very few are fortunate enough to have this oppor-

tunity. Think of how many funerals you have attended where the cere-
mony does not reflect the life of the deceased. The funeral will most
likely be the last memory your friends and loved ones will have of you,
so you are encouraged to find the deep courage it will take to plan your
funeral with your loved ones. There is even a contemporary movement
that encourages funerals and memorial services to be "celebrations of
life" as opposed to "mourning the dead." It is not the intent of this
book, or of Randy, to promote either—only to underscore the sacred-
ness of this ritual and the options available.

Your loved ones will miss you terribly. There is no eloquent way to
describe the void that someone you love leaves in you once they have
left in this manner. To this end, you have another opportunity to give
the ones you love something tangible and important to you that sym-
bolizes your relationship. This memento, typically a personal item, can
prove to be something that those who are left behind will cherish during difficult times for strength and courage. It is also used to remind
them of your love. In some cases, it is passed from generation to generation long after your departure. It is interesting to note that these
mementos are very simple and, in many cases, inexpensive items that
you either used frequently or cherished.

One of the people interviewed for this book spoke of a coffee mug that
his father used to drink from. It was a mug he bought during World
War II and was his favorite—he drank from it almost every day. He
asked his father for it before he died. His father was surprised at his
son's request and asked, "Out of all the things I have, that's what you
want?" That mug has remained in the son's office for over a decade
now and reminds him of the values that his father bestowed on him.
The son looks at it every time he feels he needs grounding or courage.

You are encouraged to take inventory of both these items and the people that mean enough to you to warrant such an honorary gift. This is

not a will, which covers items of substantial financial value. This is about the "little things" that are invaluable to you and the honoraries.

◆   ◆   ◆

Answer the following question regarding your funeral:
Where will it be (location)? _____

Who will preside? _____

Who will eulogize? _____

What music or songs will be played? _____
_____
_____

Where do you want to be buried? _____
_____

What type of casket would you like? _____
_____

If you want to be cremated, where would you like your ashes to be spread?
_____
_____
_____

Any other wishes?
_____
_____
_____
_____
_____

Below are two columns—"Item" and "To be given to." Complete the Items list first. You may want to walk around your home and look at your shelves, your closet, your drawers, your garage, your storage, your office, etc. Next, make a list of all the people important to you. This will take some time, so start right away.

Once you have completed the two lists, prioritize both the items and the people. Assign your most valuable item to your immediate family or other significant people in your life and so on.

Item	To be given to...

Item	To be given to...

Topic 6
The Loved Ones

The following excerpt is from Randy's wife, Irene:

At first, yes there was anger that this was happening. I mean you go through all kinds of emotions. Randy was sad, but he was a fighter. When Randy got depressed, I remember saying to him, "You're not dead yet!" And he heard me.

I always knew more than he did. And it was a roller-coaster ride. One week he was feeling better and results were positive and the next week it was worse. It was hard to go through those highs and lows for all of us. So I managed the communication by just updating everyone and being very even about it. I used the phrase "guarded optimism" a lot. We certainly wanted to be happy about good news, but there was also the element of protecting your emotions so you could handle the bad news when it came.

We told the girls together and, of course, everyone was devastated. But they all coped with it in their own way, and I think it is important to let people do that. We talked about death together, and I was always honest about Randy's condition. We talked almost every day. But I also imagine there are people who do not need or want to know details and timeframes and those wishes should be respected.

I am very independent and so it was not easy for me to ask for and accept help at first. But people really do want to help, and I hope others will allow that to happen. I found I was quite needy during this time and so many people came through for us—the girls and their families, Randy's and my own family and friends. It was really very touching. This experience can truly bring out the best in people.

The little things go far—even a phone call. If you were ever in the armed forces, it was mail. The best thing that could happen all week would be a letter from home or from a friend. Why? Because it showed someone cared and someone was thinking about you.

Randy and I got closer than I imagined we would, and it was not like we weren't close—we just got closer and that was special.

After he died, I went through another series of emotions, including some relief that he was not in pain anymore. It was awful to watch him be sick. I miss him terribly. Small things remind me of him constantly—they told me that family events would be hardest and I shrugged it off, but it's so true. The holidays are hard. But it's okay to reflect and be sad. Randy and I talked about life without him, about moving on, and so I am comfortable with that thought. I think it is important to talk about life without your partner if you can.

In terms of what Randy wanted through this project, I think he wanted to give hope for living one day at a time and for making the best out of that day.

For me, yes the world is different as a result of this. Randy was the outgoing one, but I have learned to be with people and the power of friendships and kindness. I think I worked too hard and worried about the wrong things—but my family and my friends are much more in my thoughts now.

◆   ◆   ◆

This book is intended for both the cancer fighter as well as his or her loved ones, so it was important to include the perspective of the primary care giver as well. In this case, Randy's wife, Irene, was that person.

As mentioned in previous topics and by Randy himself, the toll on the loved ones is enormous and allowing time for them to process their emotions and develop their own support system is highly recommended.

All the literature and people researched suggest a powerful and consistent theme during the final months of life: there seems to be a need for family—for their presence, their memories, their love, and their time. Almost all fighters seem to want to connect with relatives that they have not seen or heard from in some time, as though it's a necessary to see them to achieve closure and prepare for passing on. Closure does not mean resolution to age-old conflicts or contention; it simply but inexplicably the act of saying goodbye to one of your own. This is the power of family—that you are asked to make yourselves available to each other, as fighters and as loved ones.

Regarding the emotions after death, find comfort in Irene's heart-felt message—"It's okay to be sad—we talked about this." One conversation not to avoid should be around responses to, "So what do I do when…" If you have this dialogue, it is almost like you have been given permission to feel what you are feeling, thus allowing your emotions to cycle through you instead of bottling up inside of you.

Developing a structure for communicating to all your loved ones can be another productive time-saver. Managing communications alone can be a full-time and very stressful task. In lieu of responding to constant calls regarding updates on doctor visits and results of tests, determine a specific time each week that you will call everyone. Creating distribution lists on email for mass communiqués is another good idea. Some people have even created personal websites and kept daily entries to allow others to keep informed. You should decide collectively what is appropriate for you and your needs regarding communication.

Finally, to the loved ones, expect to transform into someone different as a result of what you are going through. Hopefully, this new person that you are becoming will be a better person who is more aware of the finality of life and the gift that the deceased has left you with. You have gained unparalleled, and perhaps never again to be experienced, knowledge and wisdom regarding life's finality and vulnerability. Take some time and allow yourself to be different and better. Be sad, but be better with those that are still around you, especially your family. No author, poet, painter or philosopher can adequately explain the power of family.

◆   ◆   ◆

How would you like your significant other(s) to live after you have passed?

_____

_____

_____

_____

_____

_____

Write down the names of some family members you would like to connect with and want to make a part of your regular communication process.

_____

_____

_____

_____

_____

_____

_____

Your communication plan:
Who are all the audiences that need to be communicated to? What are their addresses, phone numbers and email addresses?

_____

_____

_____

_____

_____

_____

_____

_____

_____

What is the most convenient communication medium for you (email, phone, writing newsletters, maintaining a website?

_____

_____

_____

_____

What time of the day or week is it most convenient for you to communicate?

_____

_____

_____

_____

What will you remember/cherish the most about this experience?

_____

_____

_____

_____

_____

_____

_____

What is your name?

_____

Who can you share this completed book with?

_____

_____

_____

_____

_____

"Our deepest fear is not that we are inadequate. Our deepest fear is that we are powerful beyond measure. It is our light, not our darkness, that most frightens us. We ask ourselves, who am I to be brilliant, gorgeous, talented and fabulous? Actually, who are you not to be? Your playing small does not serve the world. There is nothing enlightening about shrinking so that others around you won't feel insecure. It is not in just some of us; it is in everyone. And as we let our light shine, we consciously give others permission to do the same. As we are liberated from our own fear, our presence automatically liberates others."

—*Excerpt from Nelson Mandela's 1994 Inauguration Speech*

0-595-27732-2